GW01375457

my big pink book of everything

Chez Picthall & Christiane Gunzi

Picthall & Gunzi Ltd

Contents

My pink alphabet — 6
The book begins with the alphabet as children learn to identify and name all the letters.

Being busy at work — 8
The child counts objects from 1 to 10 in groups, and starts to recognise written numerals.

Some of my favourite things — 10
Higher numbers are included, as children count from 11 to 20 and match numerals to groups.

Let's have a picnic! — 12
All the main colours are shown, and children can match them up with pictures of picnic things.

Let's look at shapes! — 14
Here the child discovers flat and solid shapes, and matches each shape to an everyday object.

Created & produced by:
Picthall & Gunzi Limited
21A Widmore Road
Bromley
Kent BR1 1RW
United Kingdom

Copyright © 2005
Picthall & Gunzi Limited

Original concept: Chez Picthall
Written & edited by: Christiane Gunzi
Designer: Paul Calver
Design Assistant: Ray Bryant
Education consultants: Diana Bentley, MA Advanced Dip. in Children's Literature, & Jane Whitwell, Diploma in Special Educational Needs
Photography: Steve Gorton, Andy Crawford & Chez Picthall

All rights reserved. No part of this publication may be reproduced, stored in a retrieval system or transmitted in any form or by any means, electronic, mechanical, photocopying, recording or otherwise, without the prior written permission of the publisher.

ISBN 1-904618-35-9

Reproduction by Colourscan in Singapore
Printed & bound in Italy

Picthall & Gunzi wish to thank the following children for being models:
Lucia Allen, Isabelle Goodridge, Aliyah Green, Skye Johnson, Maria Paula Ngoyi, Yuki Price, Amber Sayers, Lily Smith & Tia Williams. Thanks also to Sue Stowers, Toby Reynolds & Gill Shaw for their help with the book.

Picture credits
KEY: b = bottom; c = centre; l = left; r = right; t = top

Courtesy of **Robert Bosch Limited**: 22tl, tr; **British Telecommunications plc**: 22cr; **Canon (UK) Ltd**: 22bl; **Deere & Company** 31bc; **Dyson**: 22c; **Frank Lane Picture Agency**: David Hosking 23bc; **Multiyork** 22bc; **NewsCast**: 22tl; **Sony UK**: 22c, 22br; **Warren Photographic**: 22br, 23tl, cl, bl, br, cr; **Woodfall Wild Images**: Adrian Dorst 26tl

Please note that every effort has been made to check the accuracy of the information contained in this book, and to credit the copyright holders correctly. Picthall & Gunzi apologise for any unintentional errors or omissions, and would be happy to include revisions to content and/or acknowledgments in subsequent editions of this book.

My favourite clothes 16
Here, children can match spots, stripes, checks and other patterns to everyday clothes.

My busy day 18
Everyday 'doing' words are introduced here, as the child is encouraged to read simple sentences.

Playing with my friends 20
The concept of grouping is explored, as children start to put objects in their correct groups.

Let's have some fairy fun! 22
The word bank on this fun page introduces the child to some useful everyday key words.

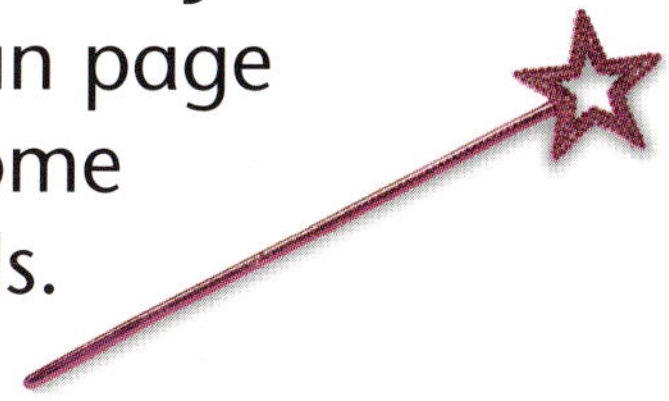

All the mermaid's friends 23
A finger tracing game on this page encourages children to associate new words with their pictures.

It's party time! 24
The concept of more and less is covered here, as children find out about sharing party things.

At the beach 26
Familiar seaside words are matched with their pictures, together with some simple sentences for children to read.

Busy in the bathroom 28
Everyday opposites, such as big and small, wet and dry, and hard and soft are all included here.

It's time for bed! 30
A word bank and maze help to extend vocabulary, and the child can do finger tracing to match up bedtime words and pictures.

Let's match pink things! 32
On this page everyone has fun matching up pictures of their favourite 'pink' things.

Notes to parents and carers

Full of fun and passionately pink, *My Big Pink Book of Everything* is a unique early-learning book created to entertain pink-mad youngsters everywhere. Using themes close to every little girl's heart, such as dressing up and parties, *My Big Pink Book of Everything* covers key maths concepts such as counting, matching, patterns, opposites, colours and shapes, building essential number recognition skills in preparation for the classroom.

Reading and word recognition skills are also encouraged, with the help of key vocabulary, word banks, finger tracing and maze games. By focussing on learning through play, *My Big Pink Book of Everything* helps to build communication, comprehension and cognitive skills, and gives children confidence as they prepare for and start their all-important first years at school.

Challenging interactive questions at the top of each page encourage communication and reading skills.

Tiny objects corresponding with every page number give extra things to seek, find and count.

Stimulating, entertaining activities throughout the book encourage children to read and count.

Bright, colourful photographs of familiar everyday objects engage the child's interest.

How to use this book
Planned with education experts and parents, *My Big Pink Book of Everything* has been devised for adults and children to dip into together, and for children to enjoy on their own. The questions at the top of each page can be used as a starting point to help you get the most out of the book when time is...

- ...some of the pages to look at when you begin reading.
- Give plenty of praise and encouragement, and always try to finish looking at the book on a positive note.
- Talk about, and look at any numbers and words that are special to your child.
- Point out numbers, pairs and groups of things when you are out and about together.
- Introduce your child to some fun activities, such as baking, which involve counting or weighing things.
- If you know any counting rhymes, why not teach them to your child?

By encouraging children to have fun with numbers and words, you will build their confidence and help them to enjoy reading and maths when they start school. As you read the book together, invite your child to look beyond the pages too, and talk about numbers, patterns, shapes and colours that you encounter every day.

Above all, have fun!

5

My pink alphabet

Let's say the letters from a to Z!
How many letters are in the alphabet?

a	b	c	d
e	f	g	h
i	j	k	l
m	n	o	p

a b c d e f g h i j k l m n o p q r s t u v w x y z

Can you find the letter p for pink?

Point to the letter g for girl!

Which of the letters spell your name?

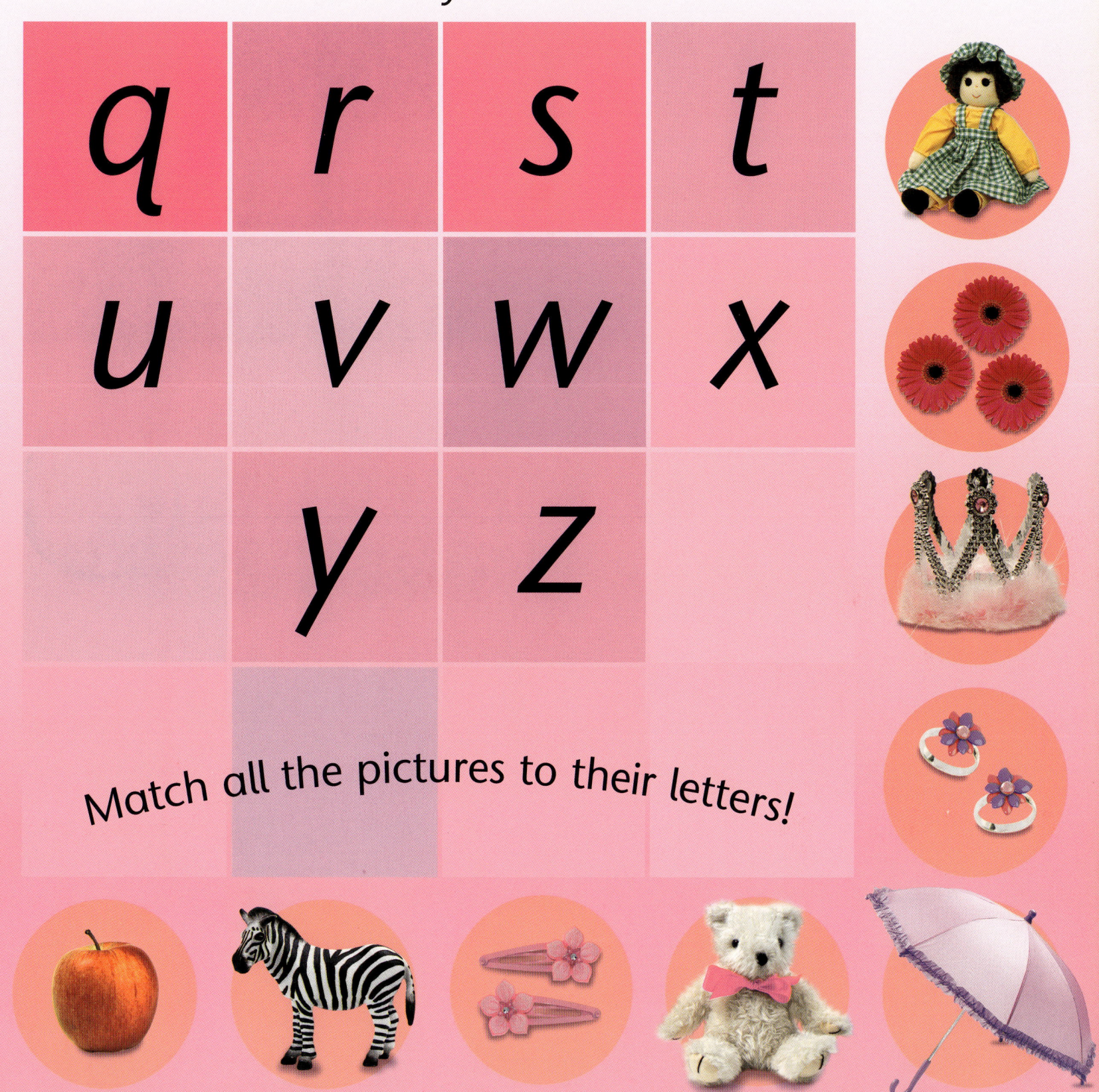

q	r	s	t
u	v	w	x
	y	z	

Match all the pictures to their letters!

A B C D E F G H I J K L M N O P Q R S T U V W X Y Z

Being busy at work
Count the pencils and find the matching number!

one notebook

two boxes

three furry pencil cases

four pads of paper

five fluffy pencils

six pencil sharpeners

1 2 3 4 5 6 7 8 9 10

How many gel pens can you count?
Count the erasers and find the matching number!
Let's count from one to ten!

seven gel pens

eight pieces of paper

nine erasers

ten paper clips

Some of my favourite things

Can you count the hair elastics?
Find the numbers from eleven to twenty!

eleven hair elastics

twelve key rings

thirteen erasers

fourteen marbles

fifteen toy animals

11 12 13 14 15

10

Count the stickers and find the matching number!
Count the felt-tip pens and find the number!
How many hair slides are there?

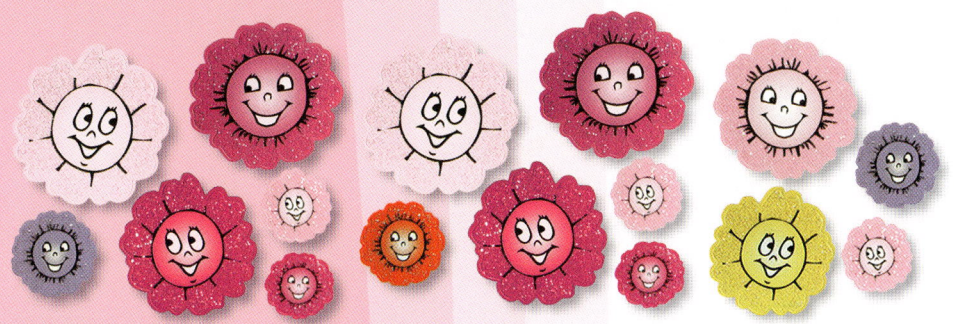

sixteen stickers

seventeen sweets

eighteen felt-tip pens

nineteen hair slides

twenty colouring pencils

16 17 18 19 20

Let's have a picnic!

How many colours can you find? Can you name all the food?

crisps

cheese

strawberries

apples

tomatoes

yogurt

biscuits

cakes

sandwiches

bread

picnic blankets

beakers

plates

| red | yellow | pink | green | orange |

12

Match all the pictures to their colours!

Find something pink!

What do you like to eat on a picnic?

doughnut

plums

cherries

chocolate

juice

hard-boiled eggs

bananas

pizza

olives

oranges

filled rolls

drinking straws

knives, forks and spoons

paper napkins

grapes

purple | blue | brown | white | black

Let's look at shapes!
Can you name all the flat shapes?
What shape is the picture of the boy?

circle

triangle

square

rectangle

oval

diamond

heart

star

envelopes

picture frame

headscarf

stickers

mirror

kite

book

chocolate coins

Can you name all the solid shapes?
Match the different objects to their shapes!
What shape is the girl's suitcase?

sphere   pyramid   cube   cylinder

rectangular prism   cone   triangular prism

mug   present

ice cream cones

candle

pencil case

box of tissues   beach ball

15

My favourite clothes

Can you name all the clothes?
Point to something striped!

vest

knickers

trainers

shorts

socks

trousers

jumper

scarf

cardigan

T-shirt

wellington boots

jeans

shoes

roll-necked top

Let's match the patterns to the clothes!
What patterns are on your clothes?

long-sleeved T-shirt

fleece

raincoat

woolly hat

belt

skirt

gloves

handbag

party dress

tights

coat

spotted

striped

flowery

checked

plain

17

My busy day

Can you see someone cooking? Match all the words to the pictures!

I am sweeping the floor.

frying pan

I am cooking breakfast.

saucepan

apron

cooker

I am planting a flower.

cakes

clothes

I am washing some clothes.

Which little girl is sweeping?

What do you like to do?

What are the other children doing?

dolls

watering can

dustpan and brush

washing machine

mixing bowl

I am making some cakes.

flower

I am pushing my dolls' pram.

19

Playing with my friends

What are these groups of children doing?

book

recorder

bucket

guitar

ball

toot toot

bang bang

parp parp

twang twang

We are playing musical instruments.

We are playing football.

How many children are in each group?
Which group does the drum belong to?
Put all the other objects in their groups!

I am drawing a picture.

I am reading my book.

We are fishing.

We are dancing to music.

saxophone

crayons

cymbals

fishing rod

drum

21

Let's have some fairy fun!

Can you help the little girl to find her fairy things? Match all the words and pictures!

lawn mower	fairy crown	keys	bath	lamp	cat	fairy lotion	clock
magic wand	aeroplane	fairy friends	television	bracelet	door	camera	fairy ring
computer	kettle	telephone	fairy dress	fire engine	fairy slippers	fairy wings	radio
dog	glitter	hair slides	window	book of wishes	sofa	fridge	vacuum cleaner

22

All the mermaid's friends
Follow the strings to match the words and pictures!

dolphins

seahorses

lobster

crab

mermaid

shells

fishes

sea urchin

23

It's party time!
How many girls are at the party?
Is there a balloon for everyone?

balloons

party hats

sweets

party blowers

fairy cakes

Can every little girl have a party hat?

Are there enough sweets for everyone?

Are there more presents than children?

masks

biscuits

milkshake

lollypops

presents

At the beach

How many sandcastles can you see?
What do these children like doing?

armbands

sandcastles | swimming goggles | starfish | sunhat | ice cream

shells | sun cream | sunglasses

I like listening to the sea in my shell.

I like digging with my spade.

I like making sandcastles.

26

Can you point to a pair of flip flops? Let's find some other pairs of things! Match the words to the pictures!

kite

rubber ring

beach ball

jelly shoes

swimsuit

spade

ice lolly

flip flops

flippers

bucket

windmill

I like wearing my pink swimsuit.

27

Busy in the bathroom

Can you name all the bathtime things?

- big sponge
- small sponge
- open box
- closed box
- short bottle
- tall bottle
- full bottle
- empty bottle
- wide comb
- narrow comb
- wet facecloth
- dry facecloth
- rough nailbrush
- smooth soap

This tap is turned on.

This tap is turned off.

28

Point to a big sponge and a small sponge!
Can you find something tall and short?
Let's find all the opposites!

straight hair

curly hair

front of the girl

back of the girl

hard bath toy

soft cotton wool

right foot

left foot

a few cotton buds

many cotton buds

new toothbrush

old toothbrush

This duck is in the water.

This duck is out of the water.

29

It's time for bed!
Follow the strings to match the words and pictures! Which child is asleep?

I am asleep in my bed.

blankets

I am brushing my teeth.

I am awake.

moon

teddy bear

I am cuddling my rabbit.

doll

30

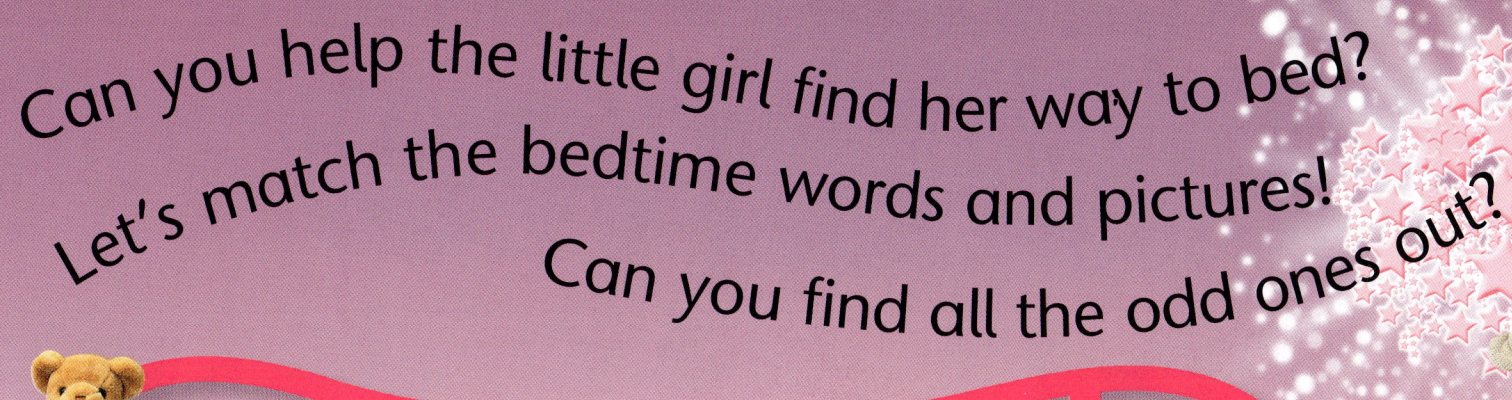

Can you help the little girl find her way to bed?
Let's match the bedtime words and pictures!
Can you find all the odd ones out?

slippers	koala	iron	pyjamas	story book	panda
car	snowman	tractor	bicycle	umbrella	wheelbarrow
pillow	girl	dressing gown	bed	teddy bear	quilt

Let's match pink things!

Can you find some pink carnations?
Match the two pink pigs! Where are the pink marshmallows?

32